THIS **JOURNAL** BELONGS TO

_____

DATE

_____

A joyful heart is like a sunshine of God's love, the hope of eternal happiness....
And if we pray, we will become that sunshine...in our own home,
the place where we live, and in the world at large.

MOTHER TERESA

PRAY·

LOVE

PRAY

LOVE

Hope is that beautiful place between the way things were
and the way things are yet to be.

PRAY

LOVE

PRAY

LOVE

Love gives, love knows, and love lasts.
JONI EARECKSON TADA

PRAY

LOVE

PRAY

LOVE

Walk softly.
Speak tenderly.
Pray fervently.

PRAY

LOVE

PRAY

LOVE

Hope is not a granted wish or a favor performed; no, it is far greater than that.
It is a zany, unpredictable dependence on a God who loves to surprise us out of our socks.

MAX LUCADO

PRAY

LOVE

Love seeks one thing only: the good of the one loved.
It leaves all the other secondary effects to take care of themselves.

THOMAS MERTON

PRAY

LOVE

PRAY

LOVE

Father, thank You for the opportunity to laugh.
Help me to find joy in everything that I do.
KIM BOYCE

PRAY

LOVE

Always believe that something amazing is about to happen.

PRAY

LOVE

Now faith, hope, love, abide these three; but the greatest of these is love.

1 CORINTHIANS 13:13 NASB

PRAY

LOVE

If there are any tears shed in heaven, they will be over the fact that we prayed so little. Heaven is full of answers to prayer for which no one ever bothered to ask.

BILLY GRAHAM

PRAY

LOVE

PRAY

LOVE

The world may be broken, but hope is not crazy.
JOHN GREEN

PRAY

LOVE

PRAY

LOVE

Love makes burdens lighter, because you divide them.
It makes joys more intense, because you share them.

PRAY

LOVE

PRAY

LOVE

Retire from the world each day to some private spot....
Learn to pray inwardly every moment.
A. W. TOZER

PRAY

LOVE

PRAY

LOVE

The moment you're ready to quit is usually the moment right before
the miracle happens. Don't give up. There is hope.

PRAY

LOVE

Love is not getting, but giving.... It is goodness and honor and peace and pure living.

HENRY VAN DYKE

PRAY

LOVE

I love the Lᴏʀᴅ because he hears my voice....
Because he bends down to listen,
I will pray as long as I have breath!

PSALM 116:1-2 NLT

PRAY

LOVE

PRAY

LOVE

When I need a dose of wonder I wait for a clear night and go look for the stars.

MADELEINE L 'ENGLE

PRAY

LOVE

PRAY

LOVE

Love is extravagant in the price it is willing to pay, the time it is willing to give,
the hardships it is willing to endure, and the strength it is willing to spend.

JONI EARECKSON TADA

PRAY

LOVE

PRAY

LOVE

You can talk to God because God listens. Your voice matters in heaven.

MAX LUCADO

PRAY

LOVE

PRAY

LOVE

God makes a promise—faith believes it,
hope anticipates it, and patience quietly awaits it.

PRAY

LOVE

PRAY

LOVE

To worship rightly is to love each other,
Each smile a hymn, each kindly deed a prayer.
JOHN GREENLEAF WHITTIER

PRAY

LOVE

PRAY-

LOVE

Slow me down, Lord.... Remind me each day...
that there is more to life than increasing its speed.
WILFERD A. PETERSON

PRAY

LOVE

PRAY

LOVE

Love is the seed of all hope. It is the enticement to trust, to risk, to try, to go on.

GLORIA GAITHER

PRAY

LOVE

PRAY

LOVE

As for me, I will always have hope.

PSALM 71:14 NIV

PRAY

LOVE

Ellie Claire® Gift & Paper Expressions
Brentwood, TN 37027
EllieClaire.com

Hope Pray Love Journal
© 2014 by Ellie Claire
Ellie Claire is a registered trademark of Worthy Media, Inc.

ISBN 978-1-60936-950-7

Compiled by Barbara Farmer

Printed in China

4 5 6 7 8 9 – 19 18 17 16 15